Tapest

Valerie Jean Mcdaniel

iUniverse, Inc.
New York   Bloomington

Tapestries

iUniverse books may be ordered through booksellers or by contacting:

iUniverse
1663 Liberty Drive
Bloomington, IN 47403
www.iuniverse.com
1-800-Authors (1-800-288-4677)

Because of the dynamic nature of the Internet, any Web addresses or links
contained in this book may have changed since publication and may no longer be
valid. The views expressed in this work are solely those of the author and do not
necessarily reflect the views of the publisher, and the publisher hereby disclaims
any responsibility for them.

ISBN: 978-1-4502-1385-1 (pbk)
ISBN: 978-1-4502-1386-8 (ebook)

Printed in the United States of America

iUniverse rev. date: 3 / 19 / 10

"Life is a tapestry; We are the wrap, angels,
the weft, God, the weaver.
Only the Weaver sees the whole design."

—Quoted in The Angels Little Instruction Book
by Eileen Elias Freeman, 1994

DEDICATION PAGE

In composing these works, I have exposed myself to many judgmental actions concerning my attitudes and responses to life.

I have been truthful in all my interactions. These tapestries consist of threads of my life. Interweaving sorrows and joys, loneliness and despair, being in and out of love these are the threads of my life as it has been.

Hopefully one might see growth and wisdom

Table of Contents

Pearl Buck

Pearl Buck, serious and popular writer, said she understood the source of creativity.

The truly creative mind in any field is no more than this, a human creature born abnormally, inhumanly sensitive.

To this person, a touch is a blow, a sound a noise, a misfortune a tragedy, joy an ecstasy, a friend a lover, a lover is god, and failure is death.

Add to this cruelly delicate organism the overpowering necessity to create, create, create.... So that without creating music,

poetry books or something of meaning,

their breath is cut off from them.

They must create, must pour out creation,

by some strange unknown urgency.

They are not really alive unless in process of creation... quote unquote...

This is the closest statement of depicting my life.

My Awakening

Someone asked me where it all began, so I decided to put it together and keep it in email. And forward to people who are interested. I am revealing things here.

How short a time span it is from June of 1998. A milestone month for me. First of all, I had a delightful friend that I had know for a space of no less than eight years. He was filled with historical knowledge. Of many peoples I think given different circumstances, he would have made the most wonderful history professor. I met him one day when I was moving from a different part of town called "Ballard". As Swedish community just outside of Seattle proper in 1991, he became a friend when he helped me move from there to my present location in Seattle. I had an interesting wide bookcase that literally fell apart once it was on the truck. Well, Greg said not to worry, he was a cabinet maker, in another time and would come over and fix it. Well, I was skeptical but what did I have to loose. He truly fixed the bookcase. In fact, in case of an earthquake, the bookcase would survive. During this interaction he and I became very close friends with daily intimate contact, not physical but very wonderfully interactive.

It was Valerie and Gregg for a long, long time and we interacted or saw one another daily, and yes, I think in my way I fell in love with him. My type of teacher personality. This interaction went on for 8 years. When one day in June I called him to see how he was doing, our "stay in touch phone call", Gregg without so much as a howdy do, says to me he has fallen in love, moved a lady into his apartment and put her on his lease. Now one has to understand the type of person I am. I realize this is a highly interactive gentleman, a sort of pied piper of ladies, he suffers from that "knight in shining armor" syndrome. Always there helping rescue young ladies in some sort of distress, I could handle that but when he closed out our friendship not speaking to me I was devastated and totally thrown to the wind. The void was horrible than other types of things propagated, exploding into my psyche. I was thinking where was I at this stage of life, was I ever going to meet people and not die of being alone.

I did not realize I was alone until that time, then a horrible thing began to occur, over thirty years ago, I was raped, I thought to myself, I'm grown! I made it out alive! So I did not even think to report it, I was in my late twenties and quite strong—so I thought...

Well now after all these years, I began to have living flashbacks, where bits and pieces of the rape experience began to explode. Unto my awakening mind, coupled with the pain of it all, I fell into one of the worst depressions I have ever experienced in my life.. I couldn't get out of bed and refused to eat (a true sign of being ill for me). Nothing but nothing ever affected my appetite on day I arose to end it all, ...but before I did I searched the ads in the UK.

Came across one seeking a plump lady, well, at the time this really described me. Some 298 pounds size 24 1/2 dress, I answered the ad, emailed the English gentleman, we conversed on line, telling him of my circumstances. He replied that it saddened him that I did not have the arms of a compassionate gentleman to just hold me, I cried, I did not see that ever happening. He said "You are telling me you want to die!"

But that is not so — you just have to learn to live. So tell you what — die, I replied "WHAT". He said , "All that is past is now gone. What is it that would actually make your life worth living.?" I replied, "Writing and having my book published, traveling the world to propagate it, and finding someone special for me." He replied, "So what's stopping you?". I said "Finances!" He said, "No way, if you follow your heart, it will be there when you need it."

Well, I started writing — it was like breathing to me. Another traumatic thing happen., I met a man in a public place who I had emailed prior to the meeting. He was so fantastic, I could not believe it!. The very image of my dreams, but during four conversation, he related that, although he was "married", he would love to be with me. Well, I have this thing — I stand in line for a lot of things, like the supermarket, post office, all you can eat restaurants, picnics, movies, but not my man! I'm funny that way! But before we left the market where we met,, he turned me around and kissed me. Well, I tell you, my dear, I had never in my life reacted to a kiss that way! It seemed as if it had released an ocean of emotion and sexual desire.

Unknown to me for many years, I released the repressed sexuality that had been dormant all these years. Now I really had a problem with this new found escalating sexual desire. Crossed between my religious beliefs and my physical needs, it took me a bit to fall back and regroup, I tried to fantasize different scenes to help me visualize what it would be like to be physically satisfied. In the meantime, I wanted to meet someone special. That was one of my goals, I felt somehow it would be someone on foreign soil. But whoever this person was I would be the best companion and lover there was. That was my promise to myself. Well, I just wanted to let you know where I'm coming from.

My Howard

This is a true account of my meeting of my late husband Howard. I believe this is my first yet unknown experience in living under the control of someone (smile).

Circa 1960, San Francisco, California, just out of the Woman' Army Corp, I was living pretty much homeless, staying in all night theatres, eating popcorn and soda, that someone would buy for me occasionally, having to go to bed, to have a night in a hotel.....I finally asked for enough money to purchase dinner and have a hotel for the night.

I was a child in a grown woman's body...had no idea how to survive...was in Frisco about three months living like this, when this gentleman approached me and out right announced to me I was going to be his wife..."Sure " I say, "Absolutely!". "Please tell me your name, so I can remember it on our anniversary," I remarked. He said, "My name is Howard and I'm serious. " Well I thought this man was out of his mind. He didn't know me and he was announcing his intentions. He smiled.

"Oh I have had you investigated and know all about you". Well he must have because he did know a lot about me. He took me by the hand and led me to his beautiful carpeted hotel room. When we entered the door he said "Let's talk, but first I want you out of those clothes", Well, " I thought" He is not completely, out of his mind. He at least wants sex. To my surprise he had me disrobe and ran bath water for me and an amazing thing, this man bathed me and touched me in ways I have never been touched before, lovingly and caressingly and softly. After he bathed me he handed me a beautiful bathrobe in my size. We lay in the bed and we talked about my dreams, which I did not many., He talked about his finding me, and why he wanted me to be his wife. I slept so peacefully feeling so protected and loved by this stranger. When I awoke the next morning, I was expecting him to throw me out, but no he said "I want you here today". I said " I need to get my meager belongings" He said, "No, you'll have no need for them". He went to the dresser and pulled out draws of clothes, all my size, all matching. they were the total look in the Sixties. We sat and had breakfast,. Then he announced his three rules, that must never be broken,

    (1) I was never to lie to him,

    (2) I was never to come home drunk,

    (3) I was to be absolutely obedient to his orders.

Because he knew what was good for me, I agreed and my lessons began by placing a book on top of my head, helping me learn to walk like a lady. Lesson one came when I used to cuss., The first time I cussed, 'wham' he slapped me across the face, I soon learned the kings English. Lesson two, if I was going to read I was going to read something worth while. The first book "The Power of Positive Thinking", I loved it. I began feeding my mind and it was so exciting, he took complete care of me.

About three months passed and I got cute and ran off to my old ways for three whole days. Finally my brain cells returned to functioning level,. I called and said, " I want to come home,". He said "Go home, get undressed, bathe and be naked in bed when I get there". I said, "Yes" and went home and did just that, Well ,my brain was not functioning again, because I figured I needed an excuse for being away. I conjured up this huge lie, where I was kidnapped, and had only escaped this very day. Howard sat there and listened patiently and then told me to lie on my stomach and I did. He removed his belt and said to me, "You are not being punished for going away for four days, or for not calling, but for lying to me". He whipped me with his belt for almost 15 minutes,

I was crying, "Please stop!" but when he did the look on his face was something I had never ever seen. He went out the door saying, "You stay in bed until I return". I was so frightened and he did not return until midnight and when his key went into the lock, I jumped not knowing what to expect., but he came over to me, sat on the bed and asked me if I loved him. I was crying, "Yes, I love you". Tears were coming out of his eyes. He said, "I had to leave before I hurt you, I never want to whip you in anger. Sometimes you are like a little girl and need a whipping, just to keep things in perspective, but tonight I almost hurt you out of anger. You lied to me and that is a sign of mistrust, and we have to have trust in order to be together", I was crying so hard and promised not to lie to him again, he kissed me gently and said "This is now forgotten. We will never bring this up again". We were married a month later and I still remember how happy, loved, protected and provided for I was and loved being under his control.

Freedom

She was frolicking, weaving about the sea shore, skipping and jumping within the edges of the foaming retreating shoreline oblivious to the thoughts of others as she continued her journey.

Yes, she was thinking all her life she had sought freedom, she felt confined to the judgments and precepts of others.

Walking that fine line like a tightrope balancing on the expectations, concepts and images of what others thought her to be. The kind of person fitting into a square box, to be categorized, shelved until needed to be exploited or taken for granted.

No matter how far she ran, how wide the space between her desire and fulfillment her spider web fine entrapment only expanded, still holding her captive to other peoples concept of who and what she is.

Freedom....

What does it constitute? The tear became apparent in her web, she finally emerged not unlike an eagle beautiful in her new found flight, now she does not have to run to be free.

She only has to be...

VJM © October 21, 1998

First Love—Dedicated to Howard

I'm walking slowly drifting on a cloud of memory and
you are there categorized

Somewhere between Fosters Café, Market Street and
the old New Yorker Hotel

You who have shown me life is for living and instilled
in me a hunger and thirst for the unique, gentle, sweet
and kind

The joy, happiness, and laughter

You were my first love and the singular place

In my heart I remain yours alone

Like pyramids of old and pharaohs reminding me of
Ancient Egypt whenever I hear soft music, walk in the
park, see pink tea roses, you are there.

Presence

I awaken from a slumber filled with dreams and expectations of new ecstasies to come. I roll about in the impression left behind from your presence in my life. Suddenly I'm aware of the very scent of your cologne, softly weaving itself about the room. The echoes of your laughter, hop scotching and bouncing off the walls of the room. Our sharing together of wonders our explorations into intimacy is stirring itself like sugar in my morning coffee. Hmmm! How fortunate I am to even know you; you who has become my wandering sage, filled with unknown wisdom. My guide, protection my very life support, as a link to a parachute opening into an amazing drifting moment. Until captured into the security of warm embraces, your face emerges into my wondrous fantasies. These short trips into another world filled with your comforting kisses and warm assurances that I finally belong, what is so amazing is your ability to emerge into and grow out from our fantasies into reality. Oh, so sweet now. Not seeking tomorrow or dwelling on yesterday. Today is filled with unknown but fulfilling desires even when not present in physical reality, like soldiers infiltrating a hidden target.

Thoughts of you invade the patterns of my mind. Coffee has become sweeter. Just raising from my slumber has become an exciting adventure. Words have new meanings, expressing delightful entrances, into remembered experiences flavors of delectable taste are intensified. Because of you, life has become livable and happiness a word to be redefined, like escaping refugees from a world of depression. We reach the border of our intimacy exploding into a new wonderful world one filled with unknown but cherished creative, innovative and exciting new beginnings just because of you.

The intricate, entwined, interweaving of the tapestry of our togetherness....life

Gypsy

A traveling prince of a runaway princess gave birth to my little

Hare with sparking eyes, a coat of gold and an abundance of shedding hair.

With a will to be cuddled, loved and held all at her own schedule and pace, but what can one do while looking at her she wins you with her beautiful face, don't try to read or open a book, she will stretch out in glorious array.

She will romp and play at 3:00 am and then sleep all day. Gently awakening me by the rubbing of a cold nose until I have risen from my bed.

After all it is seven, one must play and one must always be fed.

In the day time while languishing majestically on her window seat dispelling a quiet sort of charm.

I remember restlessly sleeping only to awaken with her curled up in my arms with a loud compelling purr, eager for attention and affection.

Right from the start God's little raindrop of love, crowding out, the aloneness that once overshadowed my heart.

As A Moth To The Fire

I'm drawn to you as a moth to the fire somehow
captured into whispered desire.
Seeking the ultimate experience, your control emanates
Falling to my knees in gleeful joy seeking to your joy,
seeking to be your toy
Your whispers infiltrates my very psyche invading the
quietness of night.
Traveling about my mind visualizing ecstasy unlimited
to find my mind letting go of things mundane.
Thinking of joys beyond life's frame, yes, I'm drawn by
some mystical flame to dance like a gypsy within the game.

Yes, yes, my thoughts explore racing with joy your
whispered lore, entangled in a web of desire.
Pulled ever closer to the fire, yet in this state I am so
free, I dare it all to belong to thee.

Vjm (c) March 14, 1999

Three Traveling Kisses

The three companion kisses born together on the lips of him to whom she seeks completion they all leaped into action not unlike soldiers.

Intent on completion of their major task to overtake and hold their objective at all cost.

They boarded a raft like the marine creatures they were drinking in the majesty of the sea air, the crossing of the channel proved worthy of their efforts, braving the storms of life undaunted as they share their particular and singular objective to land and perform their duties.

With relish emotion as commanded for their host her lover once carried with him the essence of sound another the gentleness, compassion and sensuality.

Third had the passion wrapped in a envelope of desire they all discussed their objective and plans of attack, arranged their maneuvers in systematic plans, which one would go first, second.

Of course passion would be the last so it would be the best remembered...they al hopped on board a train to rest so that their journey would not rob them of their mission

It was so important that their mission be not only completed but with strength and loving implications, after a long time they awoke. Arriving in Seattle around 2:00 am, they had to lay a plan of invasion, while the subject was in a half state between sleep and dreaming, at 3:00 am they arrived. On the wings of the cool morning air.

Kiss #1 rode into the psyche on a rainbow of color and sweetly enveloped her moving lips as she moved her tongue wetting her lips in responses she heard the sound of her loves lips and enchanting singular voice whispering sweet nothing in her ear...

Kiss #2 like a dyeing pilot bit the dust in the knowledge of mission complete.

Kiss #3 arrived and entered into her dream like state...going through the door of romance and releasing all the love and compassion sent over via her lover.
Like Kiss #1 he hurled himself into his dying maneuver and died a happy camper mission completed.

Kiss #3 having the major point of their mission as he maneuvered into her psyche and stirred up all the pent up emotional desire. Diving into her

through her thoughts he dove into her waiting lips stirring within her such desire and expectation of more intimate relations. Kiss #3 also had the ultimate weapon riding on the wings of hope. He instilled within her the ecstasy of completion of her waiting. Yes, it was wonderful she could sleep now knowing she was loved in the most intimate compassionate way.

International Situation

I was en route on a date when it dawned on me about my present situation I was playing me Irish music on my walkman.

Thinking heavily about my lost Englishman. while planning my meeting with my wild randy Scotsman, I got a call from a very dear Frenchman, and was taken out to a Mexican restaurant by the American fellow.

That catapulted my present entrance into cyberspace.

Smile, Valerie

The Gift

The beautiful moment caught me quite unaware,
drifting on the wings of dreams knowledgeable of life
not being as it seems.

I was lifted up to higher ground shouting and not
hearing a sound loosing one self in subspace leaving
pain, for another place.

Whispering of joy untold as mysteries begin to unfold
carried away in a moment of time to place unspeakable
and sublime.

Sheltered in warmth and desire, dancing within the fire,
my gift of submission given to these rewarded by being
set free.

Sitting at your feet I joyfully recline drinking in the voice
whispering you are mine.
VJM © September 24, 1999

Shadows

Was it yesterday that her steps altered becoming a
chaser of dreams dancing in expectations exhilarated
and excited yet drowning in the sea of disappointment.
Swimming to keep ones head above the undertow of
despair and aloneness.
Was it in candle lit dinners, romantic costume drama of
a bygone era, that invaded her psyche.
She whispering of hoped for interludes, regardless of
the fact she is not beautiful.
Her nights becoming clouded one night excursions into
what could have been dancing in shadows, living in
castles, that disappear with the morning tide grasping
at shadows, filmy vision of timeless joys, reflections of
happiness come and gone.
Only the shadows remain mixed with soft whispers.
Going to the sea again, the waves too unpredictable
crashing against the rocks, only the sting of pain
remains, mingled with searching for what will never be.
Shadows now have become her comfort, soft billowy,
temporary non tangible, going to the sea again to
rebuild her castle.
No don't turn on the light she would die....
VJM © August 29, 1999

My Friend Ruthie

When we first met you tugged at my mother instincts.
I all of a sudden sought to surround you with you,
protection, sheltering you seeking to hear your
wounded soul. I sought to cover your pain with a soft
blanket of warm caring. I wanted to let you taste the
joy of true loving caring, unconditional friendship. Our
friendship grew like weeds.
It flowered like buttercups on an open field, growing
naturally, nurtured slowly through many interactive
years. It became part of who I am and who you were
as a person your space. In my awareness of life has
been robbed of your essence sometimes I think you
are better off no more physical pain or illnesses to deal
with.
I view with wonder our slow unassuming interaction in
life your accomplishment allowing to open my hear to
caring in a special loving way.
Your gentle loving quality, your need, awakening my
need to be needed.
Then reality strikes a blow. I look at your picture but you
are gone.
How do I fill the void.

Love

Did you really say Love, but really meaning chains and restrictions.
Love that word has been used and abused by ages, by men wanted to express their desire upon women.

You say take me as I am, like I must accept death and taxes, but I say give me of yourself with understanding, peace and love me within the space between our souls.

You whisper of an enchanted interlude and take me to a one room flat, devoid of even one touch of decoration except perhaps the cracks in the walls brought forth from years of continuous neglect.

Yes, I believe in love and would live in a tent with companionship and closeness that edifies love, that travels through the pages of the Prophet and dances on the arm of Cyrano De Bergerac or glides down Moon River with Henry Mancini. Love that reaches the inner depth of being, with the smile of the eyes, speaking through no words have passed the lips.

Love that responds, interlocking into one another's desires, piling one stone upon another, creating building blocks, fortifying one another against the storms of line.

Love that counter balances the attitudes, the other lacks creating a complete whole you say.

I ask to much but I say, I will settle for nothing less....

VJM © 1978

Changes

Change like an eagle spreading her wings exploring
freely as her heart sings. Sweeping low, riding the
crest of a wave exhilarating, exciting, quest of the
brave, reaching never before known places, charting,
mapping, enchanting new spaces.

Each new mile, tugging at soothing balm, resting
within a wonderful calm. Connecting her by a tiny
golden chain compelling thoughts whispering here I
remain my heart singing a new song.

I have found at last where I belong.

Dreams and Aspirations

Seeking, stagnate, waiting for the end to come to what
avail?

What is the accomplishment of my life?

Other than having lived precariously in younger days.
I reach an abyss of loneliness, a caravan of my own
making carved out of fear and animosity. Controlled by
others emotions and their expectations of me.

I grasp the protection of a cloud-like blanket that affords
no real protection for self or illusions. I cling to images
of hope and desire long since expired by sheer passage
of time. I dive into my fairytale castle, where my prince
is or has always been hiding from the reality of being.

I look into the eyes of productivity and find emptiness
and despair. Yet there is hope even in the midst of
my dreams. I am always have been me, perhaps
undiscovered and yet filled with unreleased potential
bursting to come forth, being to long held captive by
the powers that be.

However I am, and will succeed.

VJM © January 23, 1996

Compassion

Her feet were unsteady as she continued to climb the crevice of the rocky shore.

Methodically, systematically she finally reached the top. The rolling sea, interweaving, attacking the rocks below. The trip up to the top was paved by too many disappointments. Coupled with uncaring, judgmental, egotistical, self-seeking entities. Her wounds were many, compiled one upon another. Chipping away at her sensitive soul.

Strange that a whole world filled with people sought their own purpose taking her kindness for weakness. Discarded her when their purpose was served. Her injured soul turned her pain inward. She could not even cry. Trembling, she was thee at the very edge of the cliff, watching but not looking at the crashing waves below. Water had always been a source of comfort for her. Soothing, refreshing, and even cleansing. This time it would bring her freedom from pain.

She reached out her arm to steady herself, when she suddenly was aware of a presence, from out of the corner of her eye it seemed an apparition. He appeared from out of the shadows and in one quick sweeping movement captured her into his arms drawing her from danger. He whispered softly to her and she collapsed into his sheltering embrace. Life is for living he whispered. Suddenly tears welled up in her eyes, he set her down away from the edge. Holding her gently but securely in his embrace, things are going to be all right. His soothing voice was whispering "I am here" . Holding her as she wept. Love was the answer but compassion was the joy of renewal

VJM © September 13, 1998

Brainstorming

Ever have a collage of ideas that seemed all at once
to appear.? Corralled by a fence of preprogrammed
thought of all the negativity one has been taught.

It seems that all we undertake to do comes with
propositioned barriers to break through. Yes, something
wonderful comes to mind, take the good and leave the
other behind.

Some barriers are meant to be and adhere to, laws such
as nature, space and gravity. Some negativity is good to
draw a line in preparation to our plan in time.

We must as a precaution examine negatives well, for
in some darkness the seed of light dwells. Planting
a seed in the dark soil, behold the roses grown with
tenderness and toil.

Without darkness light is not seen. Without rain grass
is not green. Joy is felt in reference to sorrow, failure
today is a stepping stone to success tomorrow.

Light, darkness, joy or pain, failure or success ours to
gain.

VJM © 1989

One Tiny Word

One powerful tiny word, like the atom able to split the
universe in two, divide infinity, interpret fate, direct
destiny, channel impulses, capture thoughts, create
change, establish boundaries, change directions,
catapult future, attitudes and design, split decisions.

For what could, should or would have been
IF
such a minute word to explode ones future world
with brand new, never before thought of concepts and
ideas based on circumstance in on flash second of time.
VJM © November 1, 1998

The Confinement

She was running as fast as she was able,
but no matter how fast or how quickly she tried to out
run this massive stone, cone shaped, super thick entity,
it kept pace with her.

Suddenly coming from above encircling her entire
being with a cast iron enclosure surrounding and
closing about her entire body. The force of this entity
grounded her, made her immobile.

This entity seemed to thicken and gain strength her
silent call for help was captured by the thickness of
stifled air trapped in her lungs. Unable to voice her
helpless cry, no sound came forth.

The professionals, therapists and counselors spoke
of years to help but their words did not even make a
dent. The marines were called in to use their heavy
equipment to no avail, this entity was growing
thickening by the moment. She was oblivious to the
outside world. Her thoughts, now closing in on her
pain, was unbearably helpless, entrapped inside, unable
to even call for help,. All of a sudden the phone rang.

The melodious tone infiltrated the very makings of this structure. This thick killing entity crumbles into nothingness this depression stilled by the sound of his voice....

The Call

Ring ring, ring ring,..... "Hello there"...
She drank in the essence of his enchanting voice. Like
a person on a desert finding an oasis, slipping first,
then splashing the coolness about her face, neck and
body. Emerging like a sponge, soaking to draw it all
in, riding in the midst of his voice, was his laughter
engulfing her, surrounding her in protection. Whispers
become shouts, promises of completion infiltrated her
very being, like a warm spring rain capturing rainbows
in each tiny drop, showering her in hope, renewal,
creativity, awareness of the joys of life.
Her dreams are renewed now, her thoughts racing
to push time on, yet it is time enhancing the promise,
exciting the imagination, thoughts swirling in avenue of
possibilities of completion of their mutual desire.
Yes, time has become her friend, her constant, her ally,
her preparation. Vision of completion, people are tiring
of her joy, she smiles, even if she never reaches her
destination, her journey is worth it all.

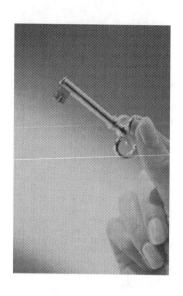

The Key

Yes!!! She thought this is the image of him. Virile, strong, handsome definitely a ladies man. What an exciting ideal thinking of their mutual satisfaction in the joining of this unusual plan.

He would be the key to release in her all the pent up desires of many years, but in so doing, she would be alive in the exchange of fantasy exploration of never-before released passion.

Yes! She thought, wetting her open lips with her tongue, he would offer his waiting embrace, she her vulnerability, their kisses would be a catalyst to desire.

Each in turn being the master of the game smiling at the though they belonged together in this shared space in time. Where he would be both King and Slave, she would be Queen and submissive. They would explore the newness of their desire basking in their mutual joys, he would show her the way, she would travel the universe of their sensuality.

Yes, he was the man, she smiled thinking once the door was opened, she would give of her intuitive imagination a spice and taste of uniqueness like salt and pepper, they were indeed a match.

She would be his in a moment, he hers in another, he was the man, but she is magical, mystical, enchanting, beguiling, WOMAN!!

VJM © September 17, 1998

Enchantment

I feel your presence in my life, influencing even my most innermost thoughts, struggling within, releasing my self from strife. Coursing through the knowledge I have been taught.

Whispering within an outdated tape. Replaying the images of a generation dream, that cannot exist in a modern landscape or survive in a polluted stream.

Yet the essence of your image does remain wandering about, seeking your particular place, shadows of the past do reclaim, the smiles within a lover's embrace.

Yes, for a time I was there all dressed in white, believing as believers do, that everything you said was absolutely right and ours the Love so true.

Now within some long forgotten dream your photograph, I with my finger retrace enchantment and laughter in your smile still gleam and strikes a pose upon your face.

VJM © April, 13, 1993

Fantasies

My life has been either one of abuse or slipping into the
mystical rounds of fantasy.

More and more now the comfort of fantasy is
overwhelming me.

Thoughts of us today, the wonderful time we will
experience and enjoy, but then as our fantasy expires
you will return to your castle in the sky and I again to
my endless search.

Diving into a sea of memories seeking joy, reciprocated
passion and unrestricted desire....

VJM © September 25, 1998

Emotions

Emotions tossed in a sea scattered about rocky crevices of life courting death. One must define life, live it, pursue it, seek its grand purpose and design. In knowledge that death is not an escape rather unknown new beginnings.

When then?

We must capture, tame and channel our wild emotions to taste, feel, experience the ecstasies and joys in transforming change each new change, like doors open to new ideas expand our haziness, broaden our knowledge enhance our awareness bringing forth the view of possibilities of living breathing life into our very dreams.

VJM © September 25, 1998

Touching

I simply hold a lot of admiration for people who can perceive, visualize, project pearls of wisdom with understanding but I for one, either from within or without must touch, perceive, interpret a mood, aura, interweaving responses with a sensual communication. A locking together of separate ideas an opening of oneself to another like being, gazing at something of eminence, delicacy and beauty.

Under glass viewing outwardly feeling robbed of the totality of it's message. A painter captures his soul, releasing pouring, expressing it through the freedom and unpredictability of the tips of his brushes. Giving it substance in splashes of color, design, preparation and image. Communicating to the world the true uniqueness, venerability, creativeness of his total being on canvas.

A singer does the same by the interpretation, infraction and melodious tones of voice, drawing images to perceive or view a vocal vision. Although songs are, for the most part, written by others, the singer in their interpretation individualizes, connects, shares one expression of thought the singer and the writer become an equation or blended unit to express, visualize, communicate one idea. So we see physically, emotionally, spiritually we must reach out to e, truly amazing, in touching we are one with the creator.

Untimely giving, receiving, perpetuating share the
identity and image of God.
VJM © September 19, 1984
Revised December 25, 1998

Attacking Thoughts

Thoughts of you as soldiers lining up to bombard the walls of my defense, catapulting stones of overflowing tenderness.

Other thoughts armed with arrows of compassion shooting high piercing my heart but the ultimate weapon a rocket filled to capacity with warm comforting sheltering embraces your sensuality.

Invades my very soul the walls of my defense have been distorted crumbling at your feet your conquest is complete.

I am your captive.
VJM © September 19, 1998

Lover's Questions

She is planting lover's questions all in a row as a
farmer's field, deeply into each furrow, hoping for a
fruitful harvest.

However, her unanswered quest drifts into the
universal awareness un-gathered, wandering into the
abyss tossed and turned as a tumbleweed on a desert
of unfulfillment.

Drifting, floating, seeking connection to her love,
life, joy and hope and by connection — completion
visualizing our togetherness as a crystal chalice,
beautiful and sparkling, Responding to the prisms of
sunlight reflecting joys of love filled to overflowing with
promise and hope.

Oh, my, to connect by the golden chains of desire and
fulfillment.
I am lost without you.

VJM © October 17, 1999

Empty House

There stands an empty house, the foreclosed sign
poised to venture in progress.
We watch in amazement at the empty house. Just
yesterday or was it years ago that our togetherness
filled each room with life living in the shadows.
Memories locked into the very corners of our living
room, kitchen, bedroom and bath. Our dreams are
floating in the misty filtering air, escaping and traveling
into the universal awareness. Our laughter and joy
invades the very plaster walls., infiltrating our senses
with the soft whispers and sounds of our voices. Our
presence is overwhelming and flooding our psyche:
kidnapping flashing moments gliding down the halls,
parting curtains, peeking into happier days.
Our memory is planted like a living vine ever expanding
and surrounding enveloping our very thoughts in this
empty house that will remain full of happiness. Camped
out on the banks of living; flowing sands of time
unmovable planted into forever.

VJM © October 28, 1998

Welcome To The Pit

Feeling so low, up is too far to go, wandering around
seven feet underground. People say they have been
there with a long vacant stare. Searching for just a
friend but the pit has no end. Just once to be able to
see the pit fraternity,. Where do they all hide? Are
they on the darker side? Perhaps we become unseen,
phantoming the dark scene. It is a time to reflect on
things and people of neglect. The outer reaches, like
moonless beaches falling then drifting into a cove until
we reach our drift, light giving us a lift but just once I
would love to see someone to share this experience
with me. Many times I have heard it said, "I love you"
after one is dead.
Each experience, fresh and new has happened to each
of you but where, oh where, does one hide, materialize
or abide now is the time to say,
"I will help you find the way."

VJM © October 29, 1992

I Am

I am that I am.

I am free! I am Free!

Not even knowing, by what chains I was bound.

The chains of self inflicted pain, despair and turmoil.

Almost a glorification of death of spirit.

Kneeling before the image of existence.

Instead of creating, living, exploring risking knowledge
of self.

Catapulting into universal thought.

Is it rebirth, rather than awareness, of who I am and
who am I.

I am that I am.

The creating of the part, that fulfills the wholeness of
the being that defines me.

VJM © January 16, 1996

My Angel (Man In A Blue Suit)

An explosion is heard in the silences of shadows, quietly I'M exploring the reaches of the universe. I am that I am lead me into new valleys, memorized by the voices of tumbling waters. A man in a royal blue suit. I have experienced his presence in times of need. He has always been, never was, and is omnipresent.

His eyes reflect the mirror of the seas. Life has sprung forth in the midst of death, releasing my spirit, not unlike a caterpillar springing forth like a butterfly. Free and able to fly above obstacles shouting in the whispers of the universe, I am free to be what God intended me to be.

Instilled within my soul is The Living Word, breathing, infiltrating into my very being. The vehicle of expression sanctioning my inner desire to be with and overtaken by agape.

Love, this light is given to me through centuries of spoken and written communication, the spirit emanates as part of me.

I am part of and contained by the universe. He is dwelling within the very essence of my being. I am reborn and part of The Living Word.

Old Photographs on 'Past Boulevard'

There I go again, traveling down 'Past Boulevard', trying to grasp some fond memory to lasso it and bring it full circle into the now.

I have not yet learned, you cannot duplicate a happy moment,. The key is to create new memories.

I'm working on it, but old photos capture the joys of my distant past.

Was I really that young, naïve, trusting, and carefree? Is the past all I really remember?

Or is it removed from the struggles incased in frames of happiness. I don't remember being that happy at the time yet the smile that is there seems genuine.

We live in shadows and reflections of what we project to others. Who really knows our true self?

The person with unkempt hair, rising naked from bed, stumbling, and reaching for her teeth, is the same polished lady in high heels and business suit, with brief case in hand, setting out to conquer another first impression, another face. But who am I but a composite of other peoples' views of me.

Rainbows

Rainbows seem to glow in the midst of spring rain, soft alluring colorful arches hopping over buildings, across from my balcony view. Basking in the joy of the light shower emanating a peaceful calmness of God's promise. He bathes the city streets with the smell of wet cement, the pitter patter of washing parked cards and tall skyscrapers.

Standing on my balcony I drink in the refreshing cleansing wetness, thinking of soft green meadows, grass standing at attention as each drop of rain infiltrates their roots. Buttercups and daisies swaying in the breeze as trees reach upward containing every nourishing drop. Weeping willow trees sheltering a warm space for lovers to be. What a loving, magnificent,, caring , protecting Father we have! Giving us His fulfilled promises or renewal and hope..

Vagabond Thoughts

Vagabond traveling thoughts carousing, settling in the lower valley of my mind, staking claim on wide spaces between hope and desire.

They seem to come along as long haired 60's troubadours, their soft voices and musical laughter infiltrating, traveling the avenues of expectation highway.

Yes, I hear them riding the tidal wave, caused by the hurricane of my dreams and desires.

Infiltrating my creativity and my inner sanction, to give me direction and help me achieve my wonderful goal.

Living life to capacity.

VJM © August 30, 1999

Seattle

This work is dedicated to Howard, my late husband. My beautiful Seattle and the beauty he showed me, just by being himself are entwined in happiness.

The crisp cool exhilarating air, with the vibrant perfume of Puget Sound, mingling with the breeze that frolics with my hair. What is the magical tie? This mystical force I feel that infiltrates and mesmerizes the very thought patterns of my mind.

Have I in reality experienced some long forgotten happiness that rolls like a tumbleweed, carousing my Seattle hills merging the sea air with the gentle falling rain.

Is my happiness so covered by time that it sleeps contentedly on First Hill, gently awakening to the cry of the troubadour poet, artist and musician whose talents and creativity mingle with smells of fresh meat and produce in the vibrant, exciting continental atmosphere of Pike Place Market?

Is not my happiness remembered laughingly imitating a pantomime clown, or playing hopscotch or skateboarding over red bricked cobbled streets, passing open air coffee shops or throwing coins in some magic fountain?

Perhaps my happiness has traveled down through dark torch lit caravans of bygone days some philosophers will no doubt sometimes say that in reality all cities are alike, but this, my city, like a citadel or castle of old spins clouds of enchantment and with the sound of her ferryboat horns beckons me to her slow, growing carefree and caring ways.

VJM © December, 1984

Animal Magnetism

He was very smooth and kind of suave with his dark
black wavy curly hair.
He smiled at her flashing white teeth and raised thick
overgrown black eyebrows.
His expression was a question of universal sexual
interaction.
Nodding his head he boarded the bus seating himself
across from her speaking with his eyes.
I was amazed and flattered as I placed my headphones
on to hear my Gospel music.
I moved down the bus and sat down. He got off the
bus but waved me a kiss as the bus pulled away. I blew
him one back.
Smiling to myself, this all because of you!

VJM © September 18, 1998

Dreams

Dreams are like soft whispers, intruding into our daily affairs, the gentle breezes softly ruffling curtains by the stairs. Fond memories truffle and sifted not unlike grapes on a vine masterly placed, by love and time refined.

Billowing in the recess of our mind, thoughts racing like dogs, nose to nose, each trying to overlap the other. Memories as projections longings of the love of another. A mothers gentle touch. A Lovers sheltering embrace.
AH!! But to live a dreamers dream that is the ultimate experience. All the great success stories far and near, drops but one precious pearl of wisdom, showering upon ones ear.

The secret of life is this,: Find what it is you love to do, pursue and perfect it your whole life through. Then you find your answer sitting by the stream of happiness entwined about success cabin, smack dab in the middle of your dream.
VJM © June 1993

Lady In Waiting

She flings back her head letting the wind sift its
fingers through her shoulder length chestnut brown
hair. Infiltrating her very being with the new found
exhilarating freedom of movement the sister of brother
wind, salts and invigorates her with the gentle spring
shower.
She stays mesmerized with feeling her eyes gazing
at the tumbling wavy water, trembling with foam.
Escaping from under the moving boat, her sliding
tongue wet her open lips each mile that parts her from
unfulfilled joy is captured in endless kisses like bottled
messages, waiting to be discovered of the chugging
tarry.
Even the sounds are countless seconds in a marriage
of endless waiting and yet within the waiting, are
the doors opening to her life, uncharted territory,
whose map she has never before sought. This journey
of awakening from a slumber turning from known
avenues, venturing almost eagerly touching life and
all it holds dear, her entire being trembles with the
expectation and longing to be brought forth.
Her very thoughts are bouncing on each wave that
separates and binds her hope. The laughter of her lover
dances upon the waves, his voice clams the unrest of

her soul, his touch will both awaken and dispel that
which she fears. Yes, the waiting is worth the gift she
inhales the sea, breathing in the exhilarating gusto
of the air. Life is returning to her body to be given
in such joy, is the ecstasy of her desire. Touch, feel
the tenderness of that sweet togetherness that will
eventually explode into unrestricted desire.
Her thoughts exploring every minute avenue of ecstasy
unexplored, she has lived for this moment.   Yes, the
waiting is worth it all.
VJM © September 1998

Solitude

'Solitude' She is here with her sister 'Contentment'. Drawing back the curtains of a guided age of treasures. Thoughts of you gather about, as crowds at a storewide clearance sale.

Grabbing, pushing, pulling, shoving their way: invading spare moments that clutter about. At intervals of inactivity in an otherwise busy day, you should have been just a memory.

Within the shelter of solitude I am mesmerized by the soft echo of your laughter. Overwhelmed by the sight of you, lost and fading, drifting backward to an unrecognized vision of what could have been.

Echoes in the Shadows

The wind is dancing playing, frolicking with her brown shoulder length hair. Her long broomstick pleated skirt and white full sleeved blouse, billowing like open sails, buffering against the flow, of streaming puffs of air, she stands perfectly still. Her foot sliding gracefully forward, but where, which direction?

Certainly not the past, nor the future, but very presently interactively entwined within the tapestry, intermingled with thoughts, desires, fantasies, hopes and dream. Failures equaling successful steps in finding the true self, that amazing inner peace, that stills the storms of life. The candle lit in darkness, that illuminates life, dispelling doubt, freeing ones soul to explore the universe.

In living, being, activating flight, as an eagle spreading her wings acknowledging sounds echoing whispers in shadows that shout, this is who I am, yes she now stands at the crossroads.
Which direction? She must follow the beating of her heart, the completion of her very soul.
The journey continues.

Georgia

Georgia is happy, almost content, not knowing where
she went, exploring avenues of reflection, healing
wounds of rejection. The boundless mountains of
pain traveling to an uncharted plane, whispering in
the deepness of night, unspeakable, unsought plight,
flashing memories here and there.

Momentary journeys into un-care invading the
thoughts of the day, like a message from some distant
bay tucked in a bottle tossed into the sea caring within
it a long forgotten please.

Years later emerging upon the scene fraying echoes of
a unheard scream, long ago wrapped in tears and fears
her cry for help fell upon deaf ears so now the message
is seeking its expression traveling through avenues of
regression.

The Dandelion and The Orchid

Memories of my Sister

I remember my sister as a three year old and I was only six months old. I remember that my sister was very abused by my mother. I remember that my sister was put in a French Catholic boarding school.

The next time I remember my sister, I was 8 years old and she was eleven. My new stepfather, Lee, had brought her home form the boarding school to live with us .

We were happy to be together again and we have many happy childhood memories but we also have difficult memories because my step-dad was an alcoholic as was my own father, George, and my mother's second husband, Jake . My sister was diagnosed as retarded but basically she was only slow to learn.

Lee was good to us and soon we had a little house.

The only problem was the drinking, the fighting, and my mother's abusive ways.

Valerie was always an "orchid" in my mind. She was delicate and easily crushed. I was a "dandelion!" Mow me down , weed me out, and I still popped up and thrived.

Valerie was destroyed by our vicious family. Although she never graduated from High School, Valerie passed a General Education test and she left home at seventeen to join the army. The following year, she was engaged but her future husband died before the wedding, then she traveled to California where she met Howard. I remember when my sister was beaten and raped during the Watts Riot. She spent several months in the hospital. She moved to Seattle and struggled there to live but she loved Seattle.

After all these years, (she is now sixty-eight) the Orchid "Valerie" is home with her sister, the Dandelion , and I am very relieved and happy

The dandelion will take care of the Orchid with the greatest of care and unconditional love.

My favorite verses in this book are 'Empty House', 'Welcome to the Pit', and "Old Photographs on "Past Boulevard'.

By VeAnn Campbell, Her Sister

About the Author

The Sky is the Limit!

"Granted that Mental Illness is often viewed as an unmovable obstacle in a persons life, Community Voices, special profile on Valerie McDaniel is unadulterated proof that there is no limit to what the human spirit can achieve. " Lu Gabriel, Reporter Community Voices Seattle Washington 1991.

About the author:

I was born in Lynn, Massachusetts on July 8, 1941 as the eldest of two girls. Because of illness as a child I did not go to elementary school but went one year to a special class. At the age of 14 I graduated from it and went directly to the 6th grade. There I became an avid reader and discovered my love for literature and poetry. I remember the first poem I read was the Highwayman by Alfred Knoes. I was so impressed that I memorized the entire poem.

Because of my lack of formal schooling my English skills such as spelling and punctuation were in need of adjustment. I graduated from Breed Jr. High School n 1958 and did one year at Classical High Night School.

From there I entered the Women's Army Corp from 1959 to 1960. I moved to my beloved Seattle in 1962 for the world's fair and my honeymoon. I graduated from Seattle Central Community College in 1995 with a 3.6 GPA. I earned a Social and Human Services degree. I worked as a Mental Health Coordinator at Harborview Hospital, Mental Health Unit in 1994 and 1995.

Since I excelled in literature and poetry I found an outlet to express my feelings in free verse and writing. For the first time in my life I was accepted for a skill I was good at. My first book "Journey's of a Moonchild" was published by Chapbook first edition in 1991. Later I published "Moonlight Reflections" first edition in 1991. I am presently working on two more books.